A Poet's Journey through England, Scotland and Wales

Written by Paul H. Tubb

www.paulhtubb.com

ISBN: 978-1-908817-79-2

A CIP catalogue for this book is available from the National Library.

Published by Original Writing Ltd., Dublin, 2012.

Printed by Clondalkin Group, Glasnevin, Dublin 11

All Poems have been tested on animals before
releasing them into the human world.

Title	Page

Title	Page

Introduction

Whilst I was out walking, October last year, trying to decide how I can poetically commemorate my ten years living in Ireland in 2012, I encountered two fellow writers. One a writer of popular fiction and the other a travel writer. At first they pretended not to see me (aren't we writers funny), but eventually we got to talking about what we were working on at the moment.

"I've just come back from a trip to the South of France, which is where my next novel is set," said the writer of popular fiction.

"Oh France, I know it well. Myself, I've just gotten back from the Bahamas," said the travel writer.

"I've been sitting in my room, writing Nonsense Verse and drawing pictures," was my contribution to this discussion.

I wondered why my writing never took me to far flung places. I should be taking advantage of being a writer and then suddenly it hit me; I rushed home and said to my wife,

"Darling, I am off to Canada. I'm going to write poetry there to celebrate being in Ireland for ten years."

"The CD racks are dusty, you said you were going to take care of them," my wife responded.

"Sweetness, I am a poet," I replied, "a free-thinker, a dreamer. I can not have my thoughts restricted by dusty CD racks. I am off to Canada."

Whilst dusting the CD racks, my wife approached me and said, "You can't go to Canada, we're due to be in England in a few weeks to visit your family."

So I decided Canada was not going happen and that I would commemorate ten years of living in Ireland by travelling to my home country of England, whilst also visiting Scotland and Wales, to write my verse.

The result is in your hands now. To prove that I was actually in England, Scotland or Wales, I wrote a Journal whilst I was there. I included it in this book.

So please allow me to introduce, 'A Poet's Nonsensical Journey through England, Scotland and Wales', a book that is part Poetry Collection, part Travel Guide and part Book hidden behind another book in a Bookshop.

I do hope you enjoy it.

Paul H. Tubb
January 2012.

All Dogs Come From Wolverhampton

All dogs come from Wolverhampton,
  I've heard that this is true.
I've been told they enter this world
  From the sports ground Molineux.*
I presume that they are created there
  In some kind of Dog Factory
And kept there till an owners found
  So they have a family.
I hear you say, "that's ridiculous.
  That just can not be so.
What on earth makes you think that?"
  I'll tell you how I know.
I've heard that dogs come from Wolves
  And Molineux is where Wolves play.
So that is proof that I am right
  And dogs are created this way.

* Pronounced Molly Knew

British Birds Don't do That

In Houghton-le-Spring,
If you hear a bird sing,
  It wouldn't be that rare I must say.
But if you see one dance
Then it must be from France
  In County Durham on holiday.
It's just too absurd
To suggest British birds
  Partake in dances of any kind.
At least not in full view,
That will never do.
  British birds are far too refined.

A Strongman from Kidwelli

A Strongman from Kidwelli said,
"I'll carry that poem for you.
It does look awfully heavy
So I'll place it on a new
Page, maybe Fifty Eight,
Or the first blank page I find.
Don't worry I'll be careful,
I'll treat it really kind."
So he picked up the Poem
I said, "Please don't do that… Stop!
It needs to be taken one word at a time
To ensure that no words

drop."

Elusive Old Man

In Newport-on-Tay
  An Old Man resides,
Although you may not know it
  As he constantly hides.
It's his hobby, he'll say
  That he'll meet you somewhere
And when you arrive
  The Old Man isn't there.
There'll just be a clue
  As to the whereabouts
Of the second clue
  That you have to work out.
And you will be wondering,
  "Where could he be?
Is it possible that
  He's in nearby Dundee?
Or further afield,
  Or closer to home?
Could he be in London,
  Or even in Rome?"
You will never find out,
  At least not until you
Solve the Old Man's
  Very last Clue.
When that is done,
  The Old Man will be there
But most people give up.

They just do not care.
McKenzie McDoon is
   The name of the Old Man.
And if you want to find him,
   Well just see if you can.

Journal Entry 1

Well my trip didn't start off as planned. I went to the airport to catch a ferry, and when I realized that I did not take ferries from the airport, I went to the port and realised I was actually meant to be travelling by plane after all, so back to the airport I went.

When I finally got to England, I discovered I'd forgotten my lucky oven glove and it would be ridiculous to suggest I travel anywhere without that. So I had to go back and do the same thing again.

I hear you ask, "What is so lucky about this particular oven glove?" Well, the first time I wore it was to remove some newly made muffins from an oven and I did not burn my hand, making me think that this was obviously something special. I then took to wearing it all the time and I never burnt my hand whilst walking down the street or sitting in a café either; offering undeniable proof that the glove is indeed lucky.

Sandra Smith

Sandra Smith was fed up,
   She wanted something banned.
She was six years old and lived
   In Stranraer in Scotland.

So what is it that upset her?
   Well you will never guess
The thing that caused her so much grief
   Was she disliked the letter 'S'

This letter, you see, seemed to start
   Just too many words in her life,
"Why do I have to live in Stranraer?
   Couldn't we move to Fife?"

"And I'm six soon to be seven,"
   Sandra continued to state,
"That's two years of the letter, 'S'
   I can't wait until I'm eight."

Her parents were really concerned
   So to make her happy they tried.
They said, "Sandra to cheer you up
   We'll take you to the seaside."

"Oh no!" shouted Sandra,
   "Anywhere but there;
What with the Sea, Sand, Shores, Shells
   And it's Stupid Sea-air."

Sandra decided to do something,
   As she was really upset.
She wrote to the Prime Minister to ask
   Him to remove 'S' from the alphabet.

But there was a problem
   As she had a point to make,
She removed all instances of, 'S',
   Which was a big mistake.

When she did receive a reply,
   From the Prime Ministers Aide,
The response was not what she wanted
   And her hopes began to fade.

It read: "Dear Mi Mith,
   I can not apologise more,
But the language contained in your letter
   We don't have a translator for."

"So nobody could read it
  And we're really sorry to say,
We'll be unable to do anything
  And send any help your way."

This presented her with a problem,
  She really was in a fix,
The number of letters in her alphabet,
  It seemed, will always be twenty-six.

So Sandra decided to give up,
  There was nothing more she could do.
The letter 'S' will play a part in her life
  Whether or not she wants it too.

Because I can't find Battleship Grey

A strange old man from Portsmouth
  Was painting his front room cerise.
But got half way through the project
  Then said, "What's the point? This must cease.
As I'll paint it again tomorrow
  Like I paint it every day.
Always an unwanted colour,
  Because I can't find Battleship grey.
So, as I can't have my favourite colour,
  The one I want this room to be,
I've taken to painting it every day,
  Some would say, quite ridiculously.
As I should be dedicating my time
  To finding the paint that I want,
So I can create the right ambience
  And mood in my room at the front."

Jeremy the Jester

For the Annual Chorlton-Cum-Hardy
　　Talent show, 'Search for a Star',
Jeremy the jester juggled
　　The contents of a jar.
It contained Mint Humbugs, but
　　What needs to be explained
Is the jar was almost empty,
　　Only two humbugs it contained;
And they were stuck together
　　Due to excessive heat.
So Jeremy's act for the talent show
　　Was juggling one, twice the size, sweet.
The humbugs he'd throw with his left hand
　　And he'd catch it with his right.
These are some of the comments
　　He received from Judges that night:
"What was that?" The first judge said,
　　"There's no talent displayed there.
Your act consisted of you just throwing
　　A sweet up in the air."
The second judge said, "My Gran can do better.
　　I know this for a fact.
She uses 3 licorice allsorts
　　For her sweet juggling act."

The third judge simply shrugged,
     Struggling to find what to say
That summed up the ghastliness of the act
     She witnessed there that day.
So Jeremy didn't progress,
     Which was what he had hoped for
He'd made a bet that he wouldn't win it
     Like he had the 5 years before.

Always in Fourth Place

There's a man from Borth,
Who always came fourth
   In the races of the local sports day,
That is held every year
And it's held very dear,
   By all the folks around Cardigan Bay.
Two years ago
He needed to slow
   Down, to a slower than normal pace,
As he almost came third
But that'd be absurd
   Because he just has to come in fourth place.

Journal Entry 2

I received a letter from a Mary, who lives in Southend. Mary wrote, "I can not tell you how much your books mean to me. I was adrift in a dull world of emptiness, now my life has meaning and joy." Unfortunately, these words were written in another letter, to another author.

The letter she wrote to me said:

Dear Poet-of-some-description,

I hear you will be coming to England soon. If you come to Southend, please do not park your car outside my house as this will block the view.

Yours blah blah blah,
Mary.

I will not be going to Southend.

The Pop Tart Lady

Mrs. Twist, from Bishops Stortford, Herts,
Has a diet that consists of Chocolate Pop Tarts
   And a thimble of water so she won't dehydrate,
   This she has in the evening at quarter past eight.
But Chocolate Pop Tarts are had all through the day,
On the floor of her living room empty wrappers lay
   As testament of her devotion to this chocolate delight,
   But she is aware that her habit isn't right.
She visit's the Doctor, who says, "Listen to me,
Your diet is in need of more variety.
   Different fruit, some fish and some vegetables,
   All eaten at three regular intervals."
She knows he's correct but she can't modify
Her diet and I will now inform you why.
   She loves her nickname, 'The Pop Tart Lady',
   Maybe she can at least change from chocolate to
                         strawberry.

You Jean

In a regular school in Wales, in the town of Bridgend,
I witnessed a conversation that drove a teacher round-the-
                                                            bend.
"Can I speak to you Jean?" Mr Montgomery asked one day.
Eugene Eccles said, "Yes Sir. What would you like to say?"
Mr. Montgomery was confused and said, "I'm not talking to
                                                            you.
I want to speak to you Jean, There's something I'd like you to
                                                            do"
Eugene hadn't grasped it and asked, "What do you require
                                                            from me?"
Jean said nothing at all, and this confused Mr Montgomery
"Not you Eugene, You Jean," he said pointing to where she sat.
Eugene replied, "I'm Eugene Sir, I can assure you of that."
This carried on like this, for an hour or more.
I won't go through the whole thing, I'm sure it'll just be a bore.
Jean never did find out, what he wanted from her.
He ended up having a breakdown, and Eugene thought, 'poor
                                                            Sir.'

The Snow Globe Repair Man of Ullapool

In a tiny shed in Ullapool,
  That's difficult to find,
Resides the snow-globe repair man
  Who really doesn't mind
People knocking upon his door,
  As long as they did bring
A broken snow globe with them,
  But if they were disturbing
Him for other reasons
  Then he will get really angry,
He will demand that you should leave
  His shed immediately.
He only cares about snow globes
  They are what he lives for,
You'll be wise to remember this
  Before you knock upon his door.
So if your snow globe's broken,
  Like for instance if you shake
Your snow globe with great vigour
  But it doesn't seem to make
The snow move in the slightest,
  By all means visit his shed,
But if you just want a friendly chat
  Try somewhere else instead…

The Cheeseburger Fairy of Littlehampton

If you find yourself in Littlehampton,
   Please keep your eyes peeled.
There's a fairy that resides there,
   In the region of Brookfield.
And she lives for granting wishes
   Whatever your hearts desire.
Like most fairies she longs to give
   People what they require.
Well that's not strictly accurate,
   You, at least, have to say please
And even then, you'll get your wish
   Only if it's a Burger with Cheese.
That's the only wish she learned how
   To grant at Fairy School.
She was normally too busy dreaming
   And acting the class fool.
So when it came to graduate,
   All that she could do
Was produce delectable cheeseburgers
   With pickles and onion too.
So if you now see this fairy type creature,
   It won't be a total surprise
And you can get a free cheeseburger,
   But you'll have to pay for your fries.

Journal Entry 3

I love the word effervescence, yet I never have used it in a poem. I realized this as I flicked through the verses already written whilst I have undertaken this journey.

I will make amends and use the word effervescence in my next few poems.

Arthur Uttlechump's statue

The minutes of the meeting,
  That was held last Saturday,
Of the Bollington Town Planners
  Are worth a read, I must say.
They spent the entire two hours
  In disagreement as to who
Was going to be the subject of
  The Cheshire towns' new statue.
There were calls for a local author
  Or one of the town's heroes,
But Betty said, "Arthur Uttlechump
  Who used to clean the town's windows.
When Arthur did his cleaning round
  My windows were so clean.
Now he's ceased, I look out my window
  And nothing can be seen.
It's thick with dirt, I'm going mad
  I don't know what to do.
So maybe Arthur will return,
  If we praise him with a statue."
But everyone else, eloquently,
  Explained why Arthur was not
The best candidate for a statue
  Considering the others they have got .
But Betty, she was adamant.

There only was one man
Who she'd consider for the statue
  And she had a cunning plan.
You see Betty was responsible
  For the provision of cakes and tea
For the meetings participants
  And everyone does agree,
That the cakes that Betty makes
  Taste exceptionally divine.
The meeting started at 7
  Betty waited until 9
When she announced, "seeing as my
  Suggestion is seen as bad,
I will not make another cake ever.
  The last ones you've just had."
The planners all looked horrified,
  The solution was now clear
Against their better judgments
  They'd agree with Betty's idea.
The vote it was unanimous,
  The statue will now be
Arthur Uttlechump's statue,
  In the town centre standing proudly.

ARTHUR
UTTLECHUMP
WINDOW CLEANER

A Womble's Call

(*Dedicated to the memory of Elizabeth Beresford*)

You will never ever guess
  What some people say is so,
When in Leachkin in Inverness,
  As a chilly wind does blow,
They say that you are able to
  Hear an unspecified
Womble's voice, but it can't be true
  As I tried and tried and tried.
I couldn't hear a Womble at all,
  Not Tomsk or Orinoco, none.
And why should you hear a Womble Call
  So far from Wimbledon Common?
So I've decided it's just a myth,
  Although as unlikely as it does seem,
On a cold night in West Turriff
  You can hear Mike Batt's Womble theme.

An old man from South Middleleaze

An old man from South Middleleaze
Longed to sail upon the seven seas.
  But Unfortunately,
  It was essential that he
Ate each day at his local Chinese.

He just couldn't break the routine
He'd done since he was seventeen.
  Each day at half four,
  Not a second before,
He would order some Szechuan Green Beans.

You can see the dilemma, I'm sure.
How can he go off and explore,
  When this action will mean
  Foregoing his routine
And what on earth would he do that for?

So although he would love to set sail,
This will be a rather boring tale.
  With no dangers, maybe,
  But tomorrow he'll be
At the restaurant at half four without fail.

Professor Dalrymple from Hay-on-wye

Professor Dalrymple from Hay-on-wye
Invented a new kind of apple pie.
  Although it was pointless, as you shall see,
  He just replaced apple with gooseberry
And made the claim it was a brand new
Innovation in apple stew.
  But everyone knew what he had done,
  "It's gooseberry pie," shouted everyone.

Journal Entry 4

I never used the word effervescence in any of my poems...

Oh well...

Bill Fripper's Play

In Hucknall on Tuesday,
  The hour I'm not sure,
I think it's in the morning,
  But I've been wrong before.
Anyway, where was I?
  Oh yes, on Tuesday
In Hucknall there's a production
  Of a very strange play,
Which was written by Bill Fripper,
  A local playwright,
Who got the idea when
  He was out flying a kite.
And that's why the play's strange
  As the idea that he got
Was, "I love flying this kite,
  I enjoy it a lot.
So if I enjoy it
  Other people, surely
Would enjoy it also
  If they could look at me.
So I'll do it on stage
  As a one man play
Called, 'Flying My Kite',
  I'm sure people will pay

To see this production,
  I know that I would.
Just a man and his Kite
  It'll be really good."
So that's it, that's his play
  As basic as ever been,
Just him and his kite and
  Someone's wind machine.
There's no dialogue, direction,
  Scenes, action or plot,
Unless you can count kite flying
  Which I think you can not.
So I won't be going,
  And neither should you,
He flies his kite most weekends
  And that's free to view.

The Idea Shop

Where do I get my ideas?
  Where do they originate?
This is a question I am asked
  At a most alarming rate.
Well I am prepared to tell you,
  With much authority,
There's a shop that sells ideas
  In Exhall near Coventry.
It's where I get them all from,
  The cost it does depend,
On how good the idea is
  And how much I've got to spend.
I bought an idea today
  And I believe it is a winner.
I'm going to get right on to it
  As soon as I've had my dinner.
It really is original,
  I think it's safe to be said.
It's about a young boy
  Who has a scar on his forehead.
His Parents are deceased and
  He lives with his mean and nasty
Aunt, Uncle and Cousin
  Who are cruel to him constantly.

So life is pretty miserable,
　But on his eleventh birthday
He discovers he's a wizard,
　When a giant comes his way
And tells him about a Wizard School
　Where he has been enrolled
Since the day of his birth
　And he's never been told
About an evil wizard…
　Well I won't reveal it all,
But I believe this bought idea
　Will be really special.
I don't believe that anyone
　Has bought this previously
So I'm going to get right on to it
　It'll be a bestseller for me.

I DON'T THINK YOUR IDEA'S AS ORIGINAL AS YOU SEEM TO.

Louise from Dumfries

Louise from Dumfries,
Kept Lanark Blue Cheese
   In a sock by the side of her bed.
Her reasoning was flawed,
As it was there to ward
   Off spirits, but sadly instead
Her friends and family
Did not want to be
   Anywhere near her room due to the stink.
She's, therefore, ghost free,
But she's also lonely
   Her strategy she should re-think.

The Canine Thespian

In Acrefair, near a main highway,
In a large pink house there lived a grey
  Dog, who had a dream, she wanted to be
  An actor like the dogs she had seen on TV.
She could act in the soaps, or in high drama,
She'd take any role to be an acting star.
  Like her hero, Lassie, she could rescue
  Anyone the film crew told her to.
She can act all tearful, or play the clown,
She could even play Snoopy, dog of Charlie Brown.
  She just wants to act and be shown on the screen.
  She acts all the time now, although she's never seen,
Even by her owner, who somehow doesn't see
When she acts around him deliberately.
  She plays dead, plays happy, she acts all upset,
  She pretends that she's ill and plays the faithful pet.
If only he'd notice then maybe they'd go
For an audition at a TV studio.
  Unfortunately, living in Acrefair,
  She's never seen TV cameras to impress there.
So she remains undiscovered, and it's really a shame
Her ability's unknown and so is her name.

Journal Entry 5

Does anyone remember the great Jaffa Cake Shortage that occurred throughout Scotland a few years ago? Probably not, whenever I ask people about this unpleasant period of history, nobody ever remembers it. I can only presume that the memory of it is too painful and they have blocked it out.

Well, the trouble with this is, as a wise man once said, those that forget history are apt to repeat it. I did not want this repeated whilst I was poetically travelling through Scotland, so I phoned up all the companies that make Jaffa cakes and asked them to make extra for my visit and ship them to Scotland.

As I enter shops in Scotland there appear to be Jaffa Cakes, so my method must have worked, even though I was told to, "get off the phone and stop being ridiculous" by many of these companies, alright 'all' of the companies.

Battenberg Breakfast of Bromsgrove

At the start of the day on the 15th of May,
  In the middle of the High Street,
The eating of Battenberg in Bromsgrove
  Is a sensation that is hard to beat.
No one is quite so sure what is
  So great about that time and day,
But the Battenberg Breakfast of Bromsgrove
  Makes many people come and stay
Within the region of Bromsgrove,
  So they can experience the sensation
Of eating lots of Battenberg as part
  Of various combinations.
Some eat theirs with mustard, some with pickled eggs,
  Others with ketchup or jam,
There are those that add sausage or onions,
  But nobody eats it with ham.
Obviously that suggestion is just too
  Ridiculous to contemplate.
Battenberg and ham should never, ever, ever,
  Ever, be on the same plate.

The Annual Pickled Onion Throwing Championship

The Annual Pickled Onion
  Throwing Championship,
Was held yesterday afternoon
  In the Somerset Village Bawdrip.
The championship is held in
  A different place every year,
Unfortunately Bawdrip is
  A place I am nowhere near.
So I am unable to tell you
  Anything that occurred,
I can't inform you who finished
  First, Second or Third.
To find out this information
  I'd suggest the local press.
Getting sporting results from poets
  Is a bad idea, I must stress.

Buns On Display

In Islip there's a café
   That's known for its iced buns.
They come in pink, white, blue and red
   And there's multicoloured ones.
They look so nice, so generally
   People feel they won't
Want to eat these works of art,
   So most of the time they don't.
But the owners don't want them wasted,
   So they won't throw these buns away,
Because they look so attractive
   The café's put them on display.
So take a trip to see these buns,
   They are no longer on sale.
But please don't take a crafty bite
   As by now they're really stale.

Sergeant McGurk

Sergeant McGurk,
From Laurencekirk,
  Would dye his thinning hair bright green
Each Thursday night.
It was a sight
  That was only believed once it's seen.

He causes a storm
In his uniform,
  Just walking around Laurencekirk
Showing off his hair,
So people did stare,
  Saying, "That colour, on him, doesn't work."

But he didn't hide,
It was with complete pride
  That he did show off his green hair.
"I think I look great,"
Is what he did state,
  "It also matches my uniform. So there."

53

Journal Entry 6

Is it me, or is the rain this year wetter than it was last year? I must ask my friend who wants to be a weatherman if this is so.

He probably won't know as he knows nothing about the weather. He went to college to study Meteorology (The study of weather) but couldn't spell it so he studied Geography instead. He had to give that up as well, when he kept getting lost on his way to the classroom.

As I sit here on the Sea-Front, wondering these particularly profound thoughts about rain, I am eating Fish and Chips soaked by the rain. I normally just add salt and vinegar, rain water does not improve the taste.

Exceptionally Unique Shop

In Uckfield, East Sussex,
    Is an exceptionally unique shop.
If ever you're in the vicinity
    It would make an interesting stop.
'Lord Finchmaster's Piccalilli
    And Doughnut Shop', it's called.
Neither of these two is sold there,
    It sells bright blue wigs for the bald.
It's owned by a famous wig maker,
    The wigs are all made by him.
Lord Finchmaster's not his real name,
    It's just a pseudonym.
It's a very difficult shop to find,
    So if you go there specifically
To look at this shop, but can't find it
    Then, please, do not blame me.

Patrick Poppleworth from Paisley

Patrick Poppleworth from Paisley,
   Whilst watching St Mirren one day,
Shouted out, "Eureka, I've got it",
   As an idea came his way.
He hurried home that instant,
   Even though they were just half way through
The first half of a Scottish Cup game,
   He had something important to do.
He had to explain his idea,
   To his entire family.
He talked to them for a whole hour,
   Whilst they all listened intently.
When he finished he did ask them,
   "Well what do you think of that?"
Nobody wanted to say anything
   It was in silence that everyone sat.
Eventually someone told him,
   That he should have stayed at the game,
The Dishwasher's already been invented,
   Its creation he's unable to claim.

Archibald Anderson

Archibald Anderson,
  From East Kilbride,
Supported the Accies
  And he always tried
To see them at Douglas Park,
  But they are no more
To be found at this ground,
  Since Nineteen Ninety-Four.
Hamilton Academicals,
  They now do play,
At New Douglas Park,
  A short distance away.
So every time Archibald
  Travels to the ground,
He discovers a supermarket
  Is now to be found
Where the ground once was
  And his memory's to blame,
As he always forgets this
  Before the next game.
Due to his memory
  He's known far and wide
As, 'Scatterbrained Archibald
  From East Kilbride.'

Leaping Postman

I wonder have you ever seen
A postman on a trampoline?
  Well, if you go to Abereiddi,
  That is what you just may see.
The postman, Dai Daniels, is renowned
For not keeping his feet upon the ground.
  In his uniform, with his bag of mail,
  He trampolines each day without fail.
In fact he has been known to not
Deliver mail because he forgot,
  As he was in a world of his own,
  Just him and his trampoline all alone.
Jumping, jumping constantly,
Up and down, repeatedly.
  So people get annoyed as they
  Realise that there'll be a delay,
Simply because of this strange hobby.
They would complain but then they'd be
  Postman-less and they all like Dai,
  They all just wish he would comply
With their wish, that he remains on the ground,
Until he's finished his daily round.

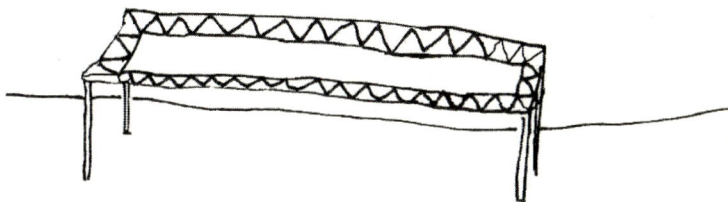

Journal Entry 7

On entry into Wales, I entered the first shop I came to and immediately began looking for Jaffa Cakes. When none were found I became erratic and upset. I located the nearest member of staff and said,

"There are no Jaffa Cakes. Do you realise what this does mean?"

"Yes. It means we are a hardware store and we do not sell Jaffa Cakes. We sell things like hammers and nails." The shopkeeper replied.

"And drills, screws and screwdrivers." Said another shopkeeper, overhearing our conversation. "If you want Jaffa Cakes, you should try Llewellyn's down the street. He sells everything." I apologized for my behaviour and I left the hardware shop and went to Llewellyn's. Not only were there Jaffa Cakes available, they were assembled in a nice looking display that looked so good I decided to take a photo of it. Unfortunately, I took a photo with a disposable camera and threw the camera away before developing the film. Oh Well...

Taking a Buffalo to the Vets

In Fintry there's a Vet
Who'll treat all kinds of pets,
   Except, because of a phobia, Buffaloes.
So poor old Major Kelse
Has to take his somewhere else,
   When he has a headache and a snuffly nose.

So he takes the Buffalo
To a Vet in Glasgow,
   Which isn't far, but can be quite a pain.
But the major does concede,
They're virtually guaranteed
   A seat when they both get on the train.

Painting Her Snails

I'll tell you something, you don't need to know,
About a girl, called Laura, from Llandudno.
  During the winter Laura never fails
  To collect and then to paint her snails.
She chooses five for her collection,
Puts them in a box for their protection.
  She paints a letter on their shells,
  A list of instructions to them she yells,
To order themselves a certain way,
Ordered, L. A. U. R. A.
  Their progress is amazingly slow,
  They still have a long way to go.
She's really annoyed at how slow they are,
So far they've spelt out ARULA.

Juggling Joanna

Juggling Joanna
　　Wore jam stained jeans
And she juggled jelly babies
　　At home in Milton Keynes.

Well not all the year.
　　I do not know why,
But only the months
　　Of June and July.

And on April 1st,
　　For one month, no more,
She'd start juggling pieces
　　Of her friends jigsaw.

That explains 3 months,
　　But what isn't clear,
Is what does she do
　　For the rest of the year?

There's 9 months of the year,
　　Where nobody knows,
Where Joanna and her
　　Strange juggling goes.

But why is this so?
    When asked to explain,
Joanna says, "I'm juggling"
    And she starts to complain.

UNICYCLE
NOT
MENTIONED
IN
THE POEM

The Kermit Carnival of Caerphilly

(Dedicated to The memory of Jim Henson)

I dressed up as Kermit, they told me to.
Got a Kermit glove puppet, which I'd bought brand
new.

I was as Kermitized as I could be,
For the Kermit carnival of Caerphilly.
I was told about it two days ago,
By a local, who said, "You really should know,
If you're in Caerphilly two days from today,
Dress as Kermit the Frog, you'll blend in that way,
As it's constant Kermit during the Carnival.
You'll blend into Caerphilly just like a local."
So I stepped out this morning in all my Kermit Gear
And noticed I was the only Muppet here.
People were pointing and laughing as well,
Saying, "How silly, he's not from here, you can tell."
So I've fallen for one of those practical jokes,
It's the last time I fall for a Muppet based hoax.

Journal Entry 8

Still have yet to use the word effervescence within one of my poems. I have decided this is due to my not having witnessed anything effervescent and I need to see something that exudes effervescence before I use the word. Unfortunately, I do not know what effervescence means. I just like the way it sounds, so therefore I am unable to use it in a sentence, let alone a poem.

I decide to purchase a dictionary with the hope that this will solve the problem.

I purchase the dictionary and look for the word, I find it and find out it means satisfactory and economical. I write the poem and read it to some random people. They tell me I should learn to use words correctly, I discover that I looked up efficient and not effervescence, which I find means excitable and bubbly. I don't think I'll use the word.

Geographical Difficulty

A poet from Ayr,
Named Eric St Clair,
   Meant to chronicle the life each day
Of a dog named Jim,
Who lived far from him,
   Upon the Bonnie Isle of Whalsay.

So, I'm sure you can see,
That this difficulty
   Meant that no chronicling was ever done.
So you're free to move through
This book, to a new
   Poem, as I'm ending this one.

IN AYR

NOTHING TO WRITE ABOUT.

ON THE ISLE OF WHALSAY

MY LIFE GOES UNDOCUMENTED.

A Green Fingered Fellow, From Bristol

A green fingered fellow, from Bristol, one day
Planted his seeds in an unusual way.
But he would never have done it, if he knew
What planting the seed this way would do.
Throughout his whole house now a jungle had grown,
As soon as he saw it he'd shout and he'd moan.
Then he'd chop and he'd cut, trying to make his way
through

This horticultured obstacle, that still grew and grew.
He stopped for a moment, to mop at his brow
And say, "Right that's it, from this moment now,
I'll stick to planting conventionally.
The days of weird methods are over for me."
Unfortunately, he's still stuck there, trying so hard
To escape from the plant that has his exit barred.
So, as he's unavailable for an interview,
I can't discover the unusual method for you.

Dubious Cures

An old man from Merthyr Tydfil
Said, "A cure for any known ill
    Is a bright yellow shoe,
    Filled with dumplings and stew
And eaten on a dark muddy hill."

"Another cure," he continued
"Is take rhubarb, recently stewed,
    And place in a sock,
    With a cube of fish stock
And then onto your bedpost it's glued."

But, please don't get carried away.
There is one thing I would like to say,
    I've tried these remedies
    And they don't work, so please,
Just stick with your Doctor, OK…

Bertram Magill

Bertram Magill,
From Muswell Hill,
Was told that movement would make him ill.

It was said in jest,
But he'd never guessed,
So to remain still since then he has done his best.

Since these words were said,
He's tried to stay in bed,
When he has to get up, movement is limited.

What's done is done,
But I wish someone
Would tell him it was only said in fun.

Then he can move too,
Just like me and you
And he'd be able to do what he wants to do.

Journal Entry 9

Whilst feeding the gorillas, in a zoo in some town north of Nottingham, but South of Glasgow, I realised the reason for the Jaffa Cake shortages... It's the puffins, they eat them. Like the old song says,

Puffins don't eat muffins
They eat Jaffa Cakes,
So don't make mistakes
By giving them muffins instead of Jaffa Cakes...

It's a really bad song, but you know what they say, "the worse the song the more likely it is based on fact..."

That would explain so much...

Holyhead... Why?

I meant to go to Holyhead,
I don't know why, but I instead
  Ended up in the town Chirk
  And then it took a lot of work
To get to where I'm meant to be.
I travelled round the whole country,
  Until to Holyhead I got,
  But, unfortunately, I could not
Remember why I needed to
Be here, what did I need to do?
  I seem to remember it was quite
  An important thing, but try as I might
My minds a blank, I do not know
And unluckily I have to leave tomorrow.

Bath Full of Pasta

An old lady from Doncaster
Bathed in a tub full of pasta.
  When asked, "Why on Earth?"
  She'd reply with some mirth,
"There's a technique I'm trying to master."

"Most people use water and soap
To clean themselves, but I hope
  That one day I'll be
  Nice, fresh and dirt-free
Using pasta, it's not worked yet, nope."

She carried on trying, of course,
But her research revealed lots of flaws.
  But she didn't quit,
  Quite the opposite,
She decided to add pasta sauce.

Fritz Snail Farm

If you see a snail,
Whilst in Kirkby Lonsdale,
   With a shell that is a pale shade of blue,
Please do not be alarmed,
This is where snails are farmed
   Snails that don't look like the others do.

The farm is called, 'Fritz
Snail farm', and it's
   Where snails, who do not fit in, go.
'Feeling unwanted is wrong,
We want snails to belong
   So, welcome all snails' is their Motto.

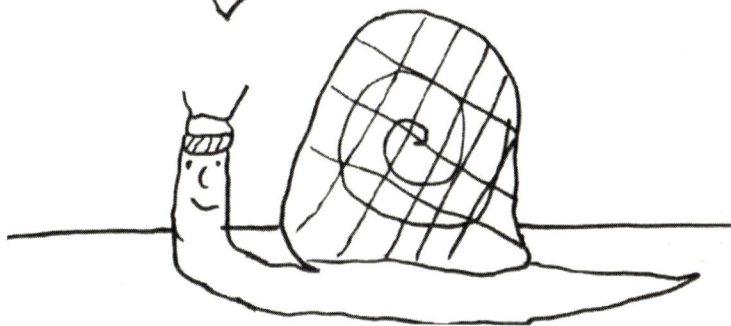

This Poem Doesn't Belong Here

In a town outside Norwich,
   Or outside Ipswich? I'm not sure.
Is it on the other coast
   Or even by the shore?
Is it in the country,
   Or is it in the town?
Is it up the country,
   Or do you have to go down?
Anyway somewhere in England,
   Is where this poem is set
And there is a point to it,
   Which I'm now going to get.
Agnes Chumpley and her dog live there
   That is all I have to say.
Maybe this subject's too sensible
   For nonsense verse anyway.

Journal Entry 10

You know what? I've actually been locked in our second bathroom for the past few months... And my wife, thinking I was in England, Scotland or Wales, has only just let me out. The conversation went something like this.

"How did you get locked in there?"

"I actually have no idea, I went in to wash my hands before leaving. The door closed and I was unable to open it. I tried shouting but the door and the walls are very thick."

"You mean to tell me you've been in here all this time?"

"Yes Sweetness."

"What about your book?"

"I'll just make it up."

So basically, don't believe a word you have read...

Acknowledgements

My thanks go to:

My Wife, Daria, for so many reasons, I can't list them all here.
My Parents and Siblings again for so much
My In-laws and all members of my family and friends…
The Late Fr. Tim Delaney
The Staff of every library and school that I've ever read at.
The organisers and staff of every Festival I've performed at.
Every Child who has ever enjoyed my poetry and song.
Every Non-Child who has ever enjoyed my poetry and song.
Sean, Sarah and all at Milk and Cookies Stories
Margo, Conal and all at Comedy Dublin.
The Gutter Book shop, Dublin.
Crispin and Simon at Footballpoets.org
Books Ireland, Inis Magazine and Carousel Guide for their kind
words about my previous books.
The Wodehouse society for publishing some of my Clerihews
and poems.
The Sherlock Holmes Society for publishing my poetry.
Children's Books Ireland for many reasons, but especially for
putting on the Children's Books Festival each year.
Poetry Society UK.
Poetry Ireland.